Christopher Columbus
And The New World Of His Discovery
Volume 1

FILSON YOUNG
[ZHINGOORA BOOKS]

About Author

Alexander Bell Filson Young was a journalist, BBC programme advisor and author. His wrote the book on Titanic, a RMS Titanic ship. His famous works includeTitanic, The Relief of Mafekingand etc.

TO THE RIGHT HON. SIR HORACE PLUNKETT, K.C.V.O., D.C.L., F.R.S.

MY DEAR HORACE,

Often while I have been studying the records of colonisation in the New World I have thought of you and your difficult work in Ireland; and I have said to myself, "What a time he would have had if he had been Viceroy of the Indies in 1493!" There, if ever, was the chance for a Department such as yours; and there, if anywhere, was the place for the Economic Man. Alas! there war only one of him; William Ires or Eyre, by name, from the county Galway; and though he fertilised the soil he did it with his blood and bones. A wonderful chance; and yet you see what came of it all. It would perhaps be stretching truth too far to say that you are trying to undo some of Columbus's work, and to stop up the hole he made in Ireland when he found a channel into which so much of what was best in the Old Country war destined to flow; for you and he have each your places in the great circle of Time and Compensation, and though you may seem to oppose one another across the centuries you are really answering the same call and working in the same vineyard. For we all set out to discover new worlds; and they are wise who realise early that human nature has roots that spread beneath the ocean bed, that neither latitude nor longitude nor time itself can change it to anything richer or stranger than what it is, and that furrows ploughed in it are furrows ploughed in the sea sand. Columbus tried to pour the wine of civilisation into very old bottles; you, more wisely, are trying to pour the old wine of our country into new bottles. Yet there is no great unlikeness between the two tasks: it is all a matter of bottling; the vintage is the same, infinite, inexhaustible, and as punctual as the sun and the seasons. It was Columbus's weakness as an administrator that he thought the bottle was everything; it is your strength that you care for the vintage, and labour to preserve its flavour and soft fire.

Yours,
FILSON YOUNG.
RUAN MINOR, September 1906.

PREFACE

The writing of historical biography is properly a work of partnership, to which public credit is awarded too often in an inverse proportion to the labours expended. One group of historians, labouring in the obscurest depths, dig and prepare the ground, searching and sifting the documentary soil with infinite labour and over an area immensely wide. They are followed by those scholars and specialists in history who give their lives to the study of a single period, and who sow literature in the furrows of research prepared by those who have preceded them. Last of all comes the essayist, or writer pure and simple, who reaps the harvest so laboriously prepared. The material lies all before him; the documents have been arranged, the immense contemporary fields of record and knowledge examined and searched for stray seeds of significance that may have blown over into them; the perspective is cleared for him, the relation of his facts to time and space and the march of human civilisation duly established; he has nothing to do but reap the field of harvest where it suits him, grind it in the wheels of whatever machinery his art is equipped with, and come before the public with the finished product. And invariably in this unequal partnership he reaps most richly who reaps latest.

I am far from putting this narrative forward as the fine and ultimate product of all the immense labour and research of the historians of Columbus; but I am anxious to excuse myself for my apparent presumption in venturing into a field which might more properly be occupied by the expert historian. It would appear that the double work of acquiring the facts of a piece of human history and of presenting them through the medium of literature can hardly ever be performed by one and the same man. A lifetime must be devoted to the one, a year or two may suffice for the other; and an entirely different set of qualities must be employed in the two tasks. I cannot make it too clear that I make no claim to have added one iota of information or one fragment of original research to the expert knowledge regarding the life of Christopher Columbus; and when I add that the chief collection of facts and documents relating to the subject, the 'Raccolta Columbiana,'—[Raccolta di Documenti e Studi Publicati dalla R. Commissione Colombiana, &c. Auspice il Ministero della Publica Istruzione. Rome, 1892-4.]—is a work consisting of more than thirty folio volumes, the general reader will be the more indulgent to me. But when a purely human interest led me some time ago to look into the literature of Columbus, I was amazed to find what seemed to me a striking disproportion between the extent of the modern historians' work on that subject and the knowledge or interest in it displayed by what we call the general reading public. I am surprised to find how many well-informed people there are whose knowledge of Columbus is comprised within two beliefs, one of them erroneous and the other doubtful: that he discovered America, and performed a trick with an egg. Americans, I think, are a little better informed on the subject than the English; perhaps because the greater part of modern critical research on the subject of Columbus has been the work of Americans. It is to bridge the immense gap existing between the labours of the historians and the indifference of the modern reader, between the Raccolta Columbiana, in fact, and the story of the egg, that I have written my narrative.

It is customary and proper to preface a work which is based entirely on the labours of other people with an acknowledgment of the sources whence it is drawn; and yet in the case of Columbus I do not know where to begin. In one way I am indebted to every serious writer who has even remotely concerned himself with the subject, from Columbus himself and Las Casas down to the editors of the Raccolta. The chain of historians has been so unbroken, the apostolic succession, so to speak, has passed with its heritage so intact from generation to generation, that the latest historian enshrines in his work the labours of all the rest. Yet there are necessarily some men whose work stands out as being more immediately seizable than that of others; in the period of whose care the lamp of inspiration has seemed to burn more brightly. In a matter of this kind I cannot pretend to be a judge, but only to state my own experience and indebtedness; and in my work I have been chiefly helped by Las Casas, indirectly of course by Ferdinand Columbus, Herrera, Oviedo, Bernaldez, Navarrete, Asensio, Mr. Payne, Mr. Harrisse, Mr. Vignaud, Mr. Winsor, Mr. Thacher, Sir Clements Markham, Professor de Lollis, and S. Salvagnini. It is thus not among the dusty archives of Seville, Genoa, or San Domingo that I have searched, but in the archive formed by the writings of modern workers. To have myself gone back to original sources, even if I had been competent to do so, would have been in the case of Columbian research but a waste of time and a doing over again what has been done already with patience, diligence, and knowledge. The historians have been committed to the austere task of finding out and examining every fact and document in connection with their subject; and many of these facts and documents are entirely without human interest except in so far as they help to establish a date, a name, or a sum of money. It has been my agreeable and lighter task to test and assay the masses of bed-rock fact thus excavated by the historians for traces of the particular ore which I have been seeking. In fact I have tried to discover, from a reverent examination of all these monographs, essays, histories, memoirs, and controversies concerning what Christopher Columbus did, what Christopher Columbus was; believing as I do that any labour by which he can be made to live again, and from the dust of more than four hundred years be brought visibly to the mind's eye, will not be entirely without use and interest. Whether I have succeeded in doing so or not I cannot be the judge; I can only say that the labour of resuscitating a man so long buried beneath mountains of untruth and controversy has some times been so formidable as to have seemed hopeless. And yet one is always tempted back by the knowledge that Christopher Columbus is not only a name, but that the human being whom we so describe did actually once live and walk in the world; did actually sail and look upon seas where we may also sail and look; did stir with his feet the indestructible dust of this old Earth, and centre in himself, as we all do, the whole interest and meaning of the Universe. Truly the most commonplace fact, yet none the less amazing; and often when in the dust of documents he has seemed most dead and unreal to me I have found courage from the entertainment of some deep or absurd reflection; such as that he did once undoubtedly, like other mortals, blink and cough and blow his nose. And if my readers could realise that fact throughout every page of this book, I should say that I had succeeded in my task.

To be more particular in my acknowledgments. In common with every modern writer on Columbus—and modern research on the history of Columbus is only thirty years old—I owe to the labours of Mr. Henry Harrisse, the chief of modern Columbian historians, the indebtedness of the gold-miner to the gold-mine. In the matters of the Toscanelli correspondence and the early years of Columbus I have followed more closely Mr. Henry Vignaud, whose work may be regarded as a continuation and reexamination —in some cases destructive—of that of Mr. Harrisse. Mr. Vignaud's work is happily not yet completed; we all look forward eagerly to the completion of that part of his 'Etudes Critiques' dealing with the second half of the Admiral's life; and Mr. Vignaud seems to me to stand higher than all modern workers in this field in the patient and fearless discovery of the truth regarding certain very controversial matters, and also in ability to give a sound and reasonable interpretation to those obscurer facts or deductions in Columbus's life that seem doomed never to be settled by the aid of documents alone. It may be unseemly in me not to acknowledge indebtedness to Washington Irving, but I cannot conscientiously do so. If I had been writing ten or fifteen years ago I might have taken his work seriously; but it is impossible that anything so one-sided, so inaccurate, so untrue to life, and so profoundly dull could continue to exist save in the absence of any critical knowledge or light on the subject. All that can be said for him is that he kept the lamp of interest in Columbus alive for English readers during the period that preceded the advent of modern critical research. Mr. Major's edition' of Columbus's letters has been freely consulted by me, as it must be by any one interested in the subject. Professor Justin Winsor's work has provided an invaluable store of ripe scholarship in matters of cosmography and geographical detail; Sir Clements Markham's book, by far the most trustworthy of modern English works on the subject, and a valuable record of the established facts in Columbus's life, has proved a sound guide in nautical matters; while the monograph of Mr. Elton, which apparently did not promise much at first, since the author has followed some untrustworthy leaders as regards his facts, proved to be full of a fragrant charm produced by the writer's knowledge of and interest in sub-tropical vegetation; and it is delightfully filled with the names of gums and spices. To Mr. Vignaud I owe special thanks, not only for the benefits of his research and of his admirable works on Columbus, but also for personal help and encouragement. Equally cordial thanks are due to Mr. John Boyd Thacher, whose work, giving as it does so large a selection of the Columbus documents both in facsimile, transliteration, and translation, is of the greatest service to every English writer on the subject of Columbus. It is the more to be regretted, since the documentary part of Mr. Thacher's work is so excellent, that in his critical studies he should have seemed to ignore some of the more important results of modern research. I am further particularly indebted to Mr. Thacher and to his publishers, Messrs. Putnam's Sons, for permission to reproduce certain illustrations in his work, and to avail myself also of his copies and translations of original Spanish and Italian documents. I have to thank Commendatore Guido Biagi, the keeper of the Laurentian Library in Florence, for his very kind help and letters of introduction to Italian librarians; Mr. Raymond Beazley, of Merton College, Oxford, for his most helpful correspondence; and Lord Dunraven for so kindly bringing, in the interests of my readers, his practical knowledge of navigation and seamanship to bear on the first voyage of Columbus. Finally my work has been helped and made possible by many intimate and personal kindnesses which, although they are not specified, are not the less deeply acknowledged.

September 1906.

CONTENTS

X THE MAN COLUMBUS

THY WAY IS THE SEA, AND THY PATH IN THE GREAT WATERS, AND THY FOOTSTEPS ARE NOT KNOWN.

THE INNER LIGHT

BOOK I.

CHAPTER I

THE STREAM OF THE WORLD

A man standing on the sea-shore is perhaps as ancient and as primitive a symbol of wonder as the mind can conceive. Beneath his feet are the stones and grasses of an element that is his own, natural to him, in some degree belonging to him, at any rate accepted by him. He has place and condition there. Above him arches a world of immense void, fleecy sailing clouds, infinite clear blueness, shapes that change and dissolve; his day comes out of it, his source of light and warmth marches across it, night falls from it; showers and dews also, and the quiet influence of stars. Strange that impalpable element must be, and for ever unattainable by him; yet with its gifts of sun and shower, its furniture of winged life that inhabits also on the friendly soil, it has links and partnerships with life as he knows it and is a complement of earthly conditions. But at his feet there lies the fringe of another element, another condition, of a vaster and more simple unity than earth or air, which the primitive man of our picture knows to be not his at all. It is fluent and unstable, yet to be touched and felt; it rises and falls, moves and frets about his very feet, as though it had a life and entity of its own, and was engaged upon some mysterious business. Unlike the silent earth and the dreaming clouds it has a voice that fills his world and, now low, now loud, echoes throughout his waking and sleeping life. Earth with her sprouting fruits behind and beneath him; sky, and larks singing, above him; before him, an eternal alien, the sea: he stands there upon the shore, arrested, wondering. He lives,—this man of our figure; he proceeds, as all must proceed, with the task and burden of life. One by one its miracles are unfolded to him; miracles of fire and cold, and pain and pleasure; the seizure of love, the terrible magic of reproduction, the sad miracle of death. He fights and lusts and endures; and, no more troubled by any wonder, sleeps at last. But throughout the days of his life, in the very act of his rude existence, this great tumultuous presence of the sea troubles and overbears him. Sometimes in its bellowing rage it terrifies him, sometimes in its tranquillity it allures him; but whatever he is doing, grubbing for roots, chipping experimentally with bones and stones, he has an eye upon it; and in his passage by the shore he pauses, looks, and wonders. His eye is led from the crumbling snow at his feet, past the clear green of the shallows, beyond the furrows of the nearer waves, to the calm blue of the distance; and in his glance there shines again that wonder, as in his breast stirs the vague longing and unrest that is the life-force of the world.

What is there beyond? It is the eternal question asked by the finite of the infinite, by the mortal of the immortal; answer to it there is none save in the unending preoccupation of life and labour. And if this old question was in truth first asked upon the sea-shore, it was asked most often and with the most painful wonder upon western shores, whence the journeying sun was seen to go down and quench himself in the sea. The generations that followed our primitive man grew fast in knowledge, and perhaps for a time wondered the less as they knew the more; but we may be sure they never ceased to wonder at what might lie beyond the sea. How much more must they have wondered if they looked west upon the waters, and saw the sun of each succeeding day sink upon a couch of glory where they could not follow? All pain aspires to oblivion, all toil to rest, all troubled discontent with what is present to what is unfamiliar and far away; and no power of knowledge and scientific fact will ever prevent human unhappiness from reaching out towards some land of dreams of which the burning brightness of a sea sunset is an image. Is it very hard to believe, then, that in that yearning towards the miracle of a sun quenched in sea distance, felt and felt again in human hearts through countless generations, the westward stream of human activity on this planet had its rise? Is it unreasonable to picture, on an earth spinning eastward, a treadmill rush of feet to follow the sinking light? The history of man's life in this world does not, at any rate, contradict us. Wisdom, discovery, art, commerce, science, civilisation have all moved west across our world; have all in their cycles followed the sun; have all, in their day of power, risen in the East and set in the West.

This stream of life has grown in force and volume with the passage of ages. It has always set from shore to sea in countless currents of adventure and speculation; but it has set most strongly from East to West. On its broad bosom the seeds of life and knowledge have been carried throughout the world. It brought the people of Tyre and Carthage to the coasts and oceans of distant worlds; it carried the English from Jutland across cold and stormy waters to the islands of their conquest; it carried the Romans across half the world; it bore the civilisation of the far East to new life and virgin western soils; it carried the new West to the old East, and is in our day bringing back again the new East to the old West. Religions, arts, tradings, philosophies, vices and laws have been borne, a strange flotsam, upon its unchanging flood. It has had its springs and neaps, its trembling high-water marks, its hour of affluence, when the world has been flooded with golden humanity; its ebb and effluence also, when it has seemed to shrink and desert the kingdoms set upon its shores. The fifteenth century in

Western Europe found it at a pause in its movements: it had brought the trade and the learning of the East to the verge of the Old World, filling the harbours of the Mediterranean with ships and the monasteries of Italy and Spain with wisdom; and in the subsequent and punctual decadence that followed this flood, there gathered in the returning tide a greater energy and volume which was to carry the Old World bodily across the ocean. And yet, for all their wisdom and power, the Spanish and Portuguese were still in the attitude of our primitive man, standing on the sea-shore and looking out in wonder across the sea.

The flood of the life-stream began to set again, and little by little to rise and inundate Western Europe, floating off the galleys and caravels of King Alphonso of Portugal, and sending them to feel their way along the coasts of Africa; a little later drawing the mind of Prince Henry the Navigator to devote his life to the conquest and possession of the unknown. In his great castle on the promontory of Sagres, with the voice of the Atlantic thundering in his ears, and its mists and sprays bounding his vision, he felt the full force of the stream, and stretched his arms to the mysterious West. But the inner light was not yet so brightly kindled that he dared to follow his heart; his ships went south and south again, to brave on each voyage the dangers and terrors that lay along the unknown African coast, until at length his captains saw the Cape of Good Hope. South and West and East were in those days confusing terms; for it was the East that men were thinking of when they set their faces to the setting sun, and it was a new road to the East that they sought when they felt their way southward along the edge of the world. But the rising tide of discovery was working in that moment, engaging the brains of innumerable sages, stirring the wonder of innumerable mariners; reaching also, little by little, to quarters less immediately concerned with the business of discovery. Ships carried the strange tidings of new coasts and new islands from port to port throughout the Mediterranean; Venetians on the lagoons, Ligurians on the busy trading wharves of Genoa, were discussing the great subject; and as the tide rose and spread, it floated one ship of life after another that was destined for the great business of adventure. Some it inspired to dream and speculate, and to do no more than that; many a heart also to brave efforts and determinations that were doomed to come to nothing and to end only in failure. And among others who felt the force and was swayed and lifted by the prevailing influence, there lived, some four and a half centuries ago, a little boy playing about the wharves of Genoa, well known to his companions as Christoforo, son of Domenico the wool-weaver, who lived in the Vico Dritto di Ponticello.

CHAPTER II

THE HOME IN GENOA

It is often hard to know how far back we should go in the ancestry of a man whose life and character we are trying to reconstruct. The life that is in him is not his own, but is mysteriously transmitted through the life of his parents; to the common stock of his family, flesh of their flesh, bone of their bone, character of their character, he has but added his own personality. However far back we go in his ancestry, there is something of him to be traced, could we but trace it; and although it soon becomes so widely scattered that no separate fraction of it seems to be recognisable, we know that, generations back, we may come upon some sympathetic fact, some reservoir of the essence that was him, in which we can find the source of many of his actions, and the clue, perhaps, to his character.

In the case of Columbus we are spared this dilemma. The past is reticent enough about the man himself; and about his ancestors it is almost silent. We know that he had a father and grandfather, as all grandsons of Adam have had; but we can be certain of very little more than that. He came of a race of Italian yeomen inhabiting the Apennine valleys; and in the vale of Fontanabuona, that runs up into the hills behind Genoa, the two streams of family from which he sprang were united. His father from one hamlet, his mother from another; the towering hills behind, the Mediterranean shining in front; love and marriage in the valley; and a little boy to come of it whose doings were to shake the world.

His family tree begins for us with his grandfather, Giovanni Colombo of Terra-Rossa, one of the hamlets in the valley—concerning whom many human facts may be inferred, but only three are certainly known; that he lived, begot children, and died. Lived, first at Terra Rossa, and afterwards upon the sea-shore at Quinto; begot children in number three—Antonio, Battestina, and Domenico, the father of our Christopher; and died, because one of the two facts in his history is that in the year 1444 he was not alive, being referred to in a legal document as quondam, or, as we should say, "the late." Of his wife, Christopher's grandmother, since she never bought or sold or witnessed anything requiring the record of legal document, history speaks no word; although doubtless some pleasant and picturesque old lady, or lady other than pleasant and picturesque, had place in the experience or imagination of young Christopher. Of the pair, old Quondam Giovanni alone survives the obliterating drift of generations, which the shores and brown slopes of Quinto al Mare, where he sat in the sun and looked about him, have also survived. Doubtless old Quondam could have told us many things about Domenico, and his over-sanguine buyings and sellings; have perhaps told us something about Christopher's environment, and cleared up our doubts concerning his first home; but he does not. He will sit in the sun there at Quinto, and sip his wine, and say his Hail Marys, and watch the sails of the feluccas leaning over the blue floor of the Mediterranean as long as you please; but of information about son or family, not a word. He is content to have survived, and triumphantly twinkles his two dates at us across the night of time. 1440, alive; 1444, not alive any longer: and so hail and farewell, Grandfather John.

Of Antonio and Battestina, the uncle and aunt of Columbus, we know next to nothing. Uncle Antonio inherited the estate of Terra-Rossa, Aunt Battestina was married in the valley; and so no more of either of them; except that Antonio, who also married, had sons, cousins of Columbus, who in after years, when he became famous, made themselves unpleasant, as poor relations will, by recalling themselves to his remembrance and suggesting that something might be done for them. I have a belief, supported by no historical fact or document, that between the families of Domenico and Antonio there was a mild cousinly feud. I believe they did not like each other. Domenico, as we shall see presently, was sanguine and venturesome, a great buyer and seller, a maker of bargains in which he generally came off second best. Antonio, who settled in Terra-Rossa, the paternal property, doubtless looked askance at these enterprises from his vantage-ground of a settled income; doubtless also, on the occasion of visits exchanged between the two families, he would comment upon the unfortunate enterprises of his brother; and as the children of both brothers grew up, they would inherit and exaggerate, as children will, this settled difference between their respective parents. This, of course, may be entirely untrue, but I think it possible, and even likely; for Columbus in after life displayed a very tender regard for members of his family, but never to our knowledge makes any reference to these cousins of his, till they send emissaries to him in his hour of triumph. At any rate, among the influences that surrounded him at Genoa we may reckon this uncle and aunt and their children—dim ghosts to us, but to him real people, who walked and spoke, and blinked their eyes and moved their limbs, like the men and women of our own time. Less of a ghost to us, though still a very shadowy and doubtful figure, is Domenico himself, Christopher's father. He at least is a man in whom we can feel a warm interest, as the one who actually begat and reared the man of our story. We shall see him later, and chiefly in difficulties; executing deeds and leases, and striking a great variety of legal attitudes, to the witnessing of which various members of his family were called in. Little enough good did they to him at the time, poor Domenico; but he was a benefactor to posterity without knowing it, and in these grave notarial documents preserved almost the only evidence that we

16

have as to the early days of his illustrious son. A kind, sanguine man, this Domenico, who, if he failed to make a good deal of money in his various enterprises, at least had some enjoyment of them, as the man who buys and sells and strikes legal attitudes in every age desires and has. He was a wool-carder by trade, but that was not enough for him; he must buy little bits of estates here and there; must even keep a tavern, where he and his wife could entertain the foreign sailors and hear the news of the world; where also, although perhaps they did not guess it, a sharp pair of ears were also listening, and a pair of round eyes gazing, and an inquisitive face set in astonishment at the strange tales that went about.

There is one fragment of fact about this Domenico that greatly enlarges our knowledge of him. He was a wool-weaver, as we know; he also kept a tavern, and no doubt justified the adventure on the plea that it would bring him customers for his woollen cloth; for your buyer and seller never lacks a reason either for his selling or buying. Presently he is buying again; this time, still with striking of legal attitudes, calling together of relations, and accompaniments of crabbed Latin notarial documents, a piece of ground in the suburbs of Genoa, consisting of scrub and undergrowth, which cannot have been of any earthly use to him. But also, according to the documents, there went some old wine-vats with the land. Domenico, taking a walk after Mass on some feast-day, sees the land and the wine-vats; thinks dimly but hopefully how old wine-vats, if of no use to any other human creature, should at least be of use to a tavern-keeper; hurries back, overpowers the perfunctory objections of his complaisant wife, and on the morrow of the feast is off to the notary's office. We may be sure the wine-vats lay and rotted there, and furnished no monetary profit to the wool-weaving tavern-keeper; but doubtless they furnished him a rich profit of another kind when he walked about his newly-acquired property, and explained what he was going to do with the wine-vats.

And besides the weaving of wool and pouring of wine and buying and selling of land, there were more human occupations, which Domenico was not the man to neglect. He had married, about the year 1450, one Susanna, a daughter of Giacomo of Fontana-Rossa, a silk weaver who lived in the hamlet near to Terra-Rossa. Domenico's father was of the more consequence of the two, for he had, as well as his home in the valley, a house at Quinto, where he probably kept a felucca for purposes of trade with Alexandria and the Islands. Perhaps the young people were married at Quinto, but if so they did not live there long, moving soon into Genoa, where Domenico could more conveniently work at his trade. The wool-weavers at that time lived in a quarter outside the old city walls, between them and the outer borders of the city, which is now occupied by the park and public gardens. Here they had their dwellings and workshops, their schools and institutions, receiving every protection and encouragement from the Signoria, who recognised the importance of the wool trade and its allied industries to Genoa. Cloth-weavers, blanket-makers, silk-weavers, and velvet-makers all lived in this quarter, and held their houses under the neighbouring abbey of San Stefano. There are two houses mentioned in documents which seem to have been in the possession of Domenico at different times. One was in the suburbs outside the Olive Gate; the other was farther in, by St. Andrew's Gate, and quite near to the sea. The house outside the Olive Gate has disappeared; and it was probably here that our Christopher first saw the light, and pleased Domenico's heart with his little cries and struggles. Neither the day nor even the year is certainly known, but there is most reason to believe that it was in the year 1451. They must have moved soon afterwards to the house in the Vico Dritto di Ponticello, No. 37, in which most of Christopher's childhood was certainly passed. This is a house close to St. Andrew's Gate, which gate still stands in a beautiful and ruinous condition.

From the new part of Genoa, and from the Via XX Settembre, you turn into the little Piazza di Ponticello just opposite the church of San Stefano. In a moment you are in old Genoa, which is to-day in appearance virtually the same as the place in which Christopher and his little brothers and sisters made the first steps of their pilgrimage through this world. If the Italian, sun has been shining fiercely upon you, in the great modern thoroughfare, you will turn into this quarter of narrow streets and high houses with grateful relief. The past seems to meet you there; and from the Piazza, gay with its little provision-shops and fruit stalls, you walk up the slope of the Vico Dritto di Ponticello, leaving the sunlight behind you, and entering the narrow street like a traveller entering a mountain gorge.

It is a very curious street this; I suppose there is no street in the world that has more character. Genoa invented sky-scrapers long before Columbus had discovered America, or America had invented steel frames for high building; but although many of the houses in the Vico Dritto di Ponticello are seven and eight storeys high, the width of the street from house-wall to house-wall does not average more than nine feet. The street is not straight, moreover; it winds a little in its ascent to the old city wall and St. Andrew's Gate, so that you do not even see the sky much as you look forward and upwards. The jutting cornices of the roofs, often beautifully decorated, come together in a medley of angles and corners that practically roof the street over; and only here and there do you see a triangle or a parallelogram of the vivid brilliant blue that is the sky. Besides being seven or eight storeys high, the houses are the narrowest in the world; I should think that their average width on the street front is ten feet. So as you walk up this street where young Christopher lived you must think of it in these three dimensions towering slices of houses, ten or twelve feet in width: a street often not more than eight and seldom more than fifteen feet in width; and the walls of the houses themselves, painted in every colour, green and pink and grey and white, and trellised with the inevitable green window-shutters of the South, standing like cliffs on each side of you seven or eight rooms high. There being so little horizontal space for the people to live there, what little there is is most economically used; and all across the tops of the houses, high above your head, the cliffs are joined by wires and clothes-lines from which thousands of brightly-dyed garments are always hanging and fluttering; higher still, where the top storeys of the houses become merged in roof, there are little patches of garden and greenery, where geraniums and delicious tangling creepers uphold thus high above the ground the fertile tradition of earth. You walk slowly up the paved street. One of its characteristics, which it shares with the old streets of most Italian towns, is that it is only used by foot-passengers, being of course too narrow for wheels; and it is paved across with flagstones from door to door, so that the feet and the voices echo pleasantly in it, and make a music of their own. Without exception the ground floor of every house is a shop—the gayest, busiest most industrious little shops in the world. There are shops for provisions, where the delightful macaroni lies in its various bins, and all kinds of frugal and nourishing foods are offered for sale. There are shops for clothes and dyed finery; there are shops for boots, where boots hang in festoons like onions outside the window—I have never seen so many boot-shops at once in my life as I saw in the streets surrounding the house of Columbus. And every shop that is not a provision-shop or a clothes-shop or a boot-shop, is a wine-shop—or at least you would think so, until you remember, after you have walked through the street, what a lot of other kinds of shops you have seen on your way. There are shops for newspapers and tobacco, for cheap jewellery, for brushes, for chairs and tables and articles of wood; there are shops with great stacks and piles of crockery; there are shops for cheese and butter and milk—indeed from this one little street in Genoa you could supply every necessary and every luxury of a humble life.

As you still go up, the street takes a slight bend; and immediately before you, you see it spanned by the lofty crumbled arch of St. Andrew's Gate, with its two mighty towers one on each side. Just as you see it you are at Columbus's house. The number is thirty-seven; it is like any of the other houses, tall and narrow; and there is a slab built into the wall above the first storey, on which is written this inscription:—

NVLLA DOMVS TITVLO DIGNIOR HEIC PATERNIS IN AEDIBV CHRISTOPHORVS COLVMBVS PVERITIAM PRIMAMQVE IVVENTAM TRANSEGIT

You stop and look at it; and presently you become conscious of a difference between it and all the other houses. They are all alert, busy, noisy, crowded with life in every storey, oozing vitality from every window; but of all the narrow vertical strips that make up the houses of the street, this strip numbered thirty-seven is empty, silent, and dead. The shutters veil its windows; within it is dark, empty of furniture, and inhabited only by a memory and a spirit. It is a strange place in which to stand and to think of all that has happened since the man of our thoughts looked forth from these windows, a common little boy. The world is very much alive in the Vico Dritto di Ponticello; the little freshet of life that flows there flows loud and incessant; and yet into what oceans of death and silence has it not poured since it carried forth Christopher on its stream! One thinks of the continent of that New World that he discovered, and all the teeming millions of human lives that have sprung up and died down, and sprung up again, and spread and increased there; all the ploughs that have driven into its soil, the harvests that have ripened, the waving acres and miles of grain that have answered the call of Spring and Autumn since first the bow of his boat grated on the shore of Guanahani. And yet of the two scenes this narrow shuttered house in a bye-street of Genoa is at once the more wonderful and more credible; for it contains the elements of the other. Walls and floors and a roof, a place to eat and sleep in, a place to work and found a family, and give tangible environment to a human soul—there is all human enterprise and discovery, effort, adventure, and life in that.

If Christopher wanted to go down to the sea he would have to pass under the Gate of St. Andrew, with the old prison, now pulled down to make room for the modern buildings, on his right, and go down the Salita del Prione, which is a continuation of the Vico Dritto di Ponticello. It slopes downwards from the Gate as the first street sloped upwards to it; and it contains the same assortment of shops and of houses, the same mixture of handicrafts and industries, as were seen in the Vico Dritto di Ponticello. Presently he would come to the Piazza dell' Erbe, where there is no grass, but only a pleasant circle of little houses and shops, with already a smack of the sea in them, chiefly suggested by the shops of instrument-makers, where to-day there are compasses and sextants and chronometers. Out of the Piazza you come down the Via di San Donato and into the Piazza of that name, where for over nine centuries the church of San Donato has faced the sun and the weather. From there Christopher's young feet would follow the winding Via di San Bernato, a street also inhabited by craftsmen and workers in wood and metal; and at the last turn of it, a gash of blue between the two cliffwalls of houses, you see the Mediterranean.

Here, then, between the narrow little house by the Gate and the clamour and business of the sea-front, our Christopher's feet carried him daily during some part of his childish life. What else he did, what he thought and felt, what little reflections he had, are but matters of conjecture. Genoa will tell you nothing more. You may walk over the very spot where he was born; you may unconsciously tread in the track of his vanished feet; you may wander about the wharves of the city, and see the ships loading and unloading—different ships, but still trafficking in commodities not greatly different from those of his day; you may climb the heights behind Genoa, and look out upon the great curving Gulf from Porto Fino to where the Cape of the western Riviera dips into the sea; you may walk along the coast to Savona, where Domenico had one of his many habitations, where he kept the tavern, and whither Christopher's young feet must also have walked; and you may come back and search again in the harbour, from the old Mole and the Bank of St. George to where the port and quays stretch away to the medley of sailing-ships and steamers; but you will not find any sign or trace of Christopher. No echo of the little voice that shrilled in the narrow street sounds in the Vico Dritto; the houses stand gaunt and straight, with a brilliant strip of blue sky between their roofs and the cool street beneath; but they give you nothing of what you seek. If you see a little figure running towards you in a blue smock, the head fair-haired, the face blue-eyed and a little freckled with the strong sunshine, it is not a real figure; it is a child of your dreams and a ghost of the past. You may chase him while he runs about the wharves and stumbles over the ropes, but you will never catch him. He runs before you, zigzagging over the cobbles, up the sunny street, into the narrow house; out again, running now towards the Duomo, hiding in the porch of San Stefano, where the weavers held their meetings; back again along the wharves; surely he is hiding behind that mooring-post! But you look, and he is not there—nothing but the old harbour dust that the wind stirs into a little eddy while you look. For he belongs not to you or me, this child; he is not yet enslaved to the great purpose, not yet caught up into the machinery of life. His eye has not yet caught the fire of the sun setting on a western sea; he is still free and happy, and belongs only to those who love him. Father and mother, brothers Bartolomeo and Giacomo, sister Biancinetta, aunts, uncles, and cousins possibly, and possibly for a little while an old grandmother at Quinto—these were the people to whom that child belonged. The little life of his first decade, unviolated by documents or history, lives happily in our dreams, as blank as sunshine.

CHAPTER III

YOUNG CHRISTOPHER

Christopher was fourteen years old when he first went to sea. That is his own statement, and it is one of the few of his autobiographical utterances that we need not doubt. From it, and from a knowledge of certain other dates, we are able to construct some vague picture of his doings before he left Italy and settled in Portugal. Already in his young heart he was feeling the influence that was to direct and shape his destiny; already, towards his home in Genoa, long ripples from the commotion of maritime adventure in the West were beginning to spread. At the age of ten he was apprenticed to his father, who undertook, according to the indentures, to provide him with board and lodging, a blue gabardine and a pair of good shoes, and various other matters in return for his service. But there is no reason to suppose that he ever occupied himself very much with wool-weaving. He had a vocation quite other than that, and if he ever did make any cloth there must have been some strange thoughts and imaginings woven into it, as he plied the shuttle. Most of his biographers, relying upon a doubtful statement in the life of him written by his son Ferdinand, would have us send him at the age of twelve to the distant University of Pavia, there, poor mite, to sit at the feet of learned professors studying Latin, mathematics, and cosmography; but fortunately it is not necessary to believe so improbable a statement. What is much more likely about his education—for education he had, although not of the superior kind with which he has been credited—is that in the blank, sunny time of his childhood he was sent to one of the excellent schools established by the weavers in their own quarter, and that there or afterwards he came under some influence, both religious and learned, which stamped him the practical visionary that he remained throughout his life. Thereafter, between his sea voyagings and expeditions about the Mediterranean coasts, he no doubt acquired knowledge in the only really practical way that it can be acquired; that is to say, he received it as and when he needed it. What we know is that he had in later life some knowledge of the works of Aristotle, Julius Caesar, Seneca, Pliny, and Ptolemy; of Ahmet-Ben-Kothair the Arabic astronomer, Rochid the Arabian, and the Rabbi Samuel the Jew; of Isadore the Spaniard, and Bede and Scotus the Britons; of Strabo the German, Gerson the Frenchman, and Nicolaus de Lira the Italian. These names cover a wide range, but they do not imply university education. Some of them merely suggest acquaintance with the 'Imago Mundi'; others imply that selective faculty, the power of choosing what can help a man's purpose and of rejecting what is useless to it, that is one of the marks of genius, and an outward sign of the inner light.

We must think of him, then, at school in Genoa, grinding out the tasks that are the common heritage of all small boys; working a little at the weaving, interestedly enough at first, no doubt, while the importance of having a loom appealed to him, but also no doubt rapidly cooling off in his enthusiasm as the pastime became a task, and the restriction of indoor life began to be felt. For if ever there was a little boy who loved to idle about the wharves and docks, here was that little boy. It was here, while he wandered about the crowded quays and listened to the medley of talk among the foreign sailors, and looked beyond the masts of the ships into the blue distance of the sea, that the desire to wander and go abroad upon the face of the waters must first have stirred in his heart. The wharves of Genoa in those days combined in themselves all the richness of romance and adventure, buccaneering, trading, and treasure-snatching, that has ever crowded the pages of romance. There were galleys and caravels, barques and feluccas, pinnaces and caraccas. There were slaves in the galleys, and bowmen to keep the slaves in subjection. There were dark-bearded Spaniards, fair-haired Englishmen; there were Greeks, and Indians, and Portuguese. The bales of goods on the harbour-side were eloquent of distant lands, and furnished object lessons in the only geography that young Christopher was likely to be learning. There was cotton from Egypt, and tin and lead from Southampton. There were butts of Malmsey from Candia; aloes and cassia and spices from Socotra; rhubarb from Persia; silk from India; wool from Damascus, raw wool also from Calais and Norwich. No wonder if the little house in the Vico Dritto di Ponticello became too narrow for the boy; and no wonder that at the age of fourteen he was able to have his way, and go to sea. One can imagine him gradually acquiring an influence over his father, Domenico, as his will grew stronger and firmer—he with one grand object in life, Domenico with none; he with a single clear purpose, and Domenico with innumerable cloudy ones. And so, on some day in the distant past, there were farewells and anxious hearts in the weaver's house, and Christopher, member of the crew of some trading caravel or felucca, a diminishing object to the wet eyes of his mother, sailed away, and faded into the blue distance.

They had lost him, although perhaps they did not realise it; from the moment of his first voyage the sea claimed him as her own. Widening horizons, slatting of cords and sails in the wind, storms and stars and strange landfalls and long idle calms, thunder of surges, tingle of spray, and eternal labouring and threshing and cleaving of infinite waters—these were to be his portion and true home hereafter. Attendances at Court, conferences with learned monks and bishops, sojourns on lonely islands, love under stars in the gay, sun-smitten Spanish towns, governings and parleyings in distant, undreamed-of lands —these were to be but incidents in his true life, which was to be fulfilled in the solitude of sea watches.

When he left his home on this first voyage, he took with him one other thing besides the restless longing to escape beyond the line of sea and sky. Let us mark well this possession of his, for it was his companion and guiding-star throughout a long and difficult life, his chart and compass, astrolabe and anchor, in one. Religion has in our days fallen into decay among men of intellect and achievement. The world has thrown it, like a worn garment or an old skin, from off its body, the thing itself being no longer real and alive, and in harmony with the life of an age that struggles towards a different kind of truth. It is hard, therefore, for us to understand exactly how the religion of Columbus entered so deeply into his life and brooded so widely over his thoughts.

Hardest of all is it for people whose only experience of religion is of Puritan inheritance to comprehend how, in the fifteenth century, the strong intellect was strengthened, and the stout heart fortified, by the thought of hosts of saints and angels hovering above a man's incomings and outgoings to guide and protect him. Yet in an age that really had the gift of faith, in which religion was real and vital, and part of the business of every man's daily life; in which it stood honoured in the world, loaded with riches, crowned with learning, wielding government both temporal and spiritual, it was a very brave panoply for the soul of man. The little boy in Genoa, with the fair hair and blue eyes and grave freckled face that made him remarkable among his dark companions, had no doubt early received and accepted the vast mysteries of the Christian faith; and as that other mystery began to grow in his mind, and that idea of worlds that might lie beyond the sea-line began to take shape in his thoughts, he found in the holy wisdom of the prophets, and the inspired writings of the fathers, a continual confirmation of his faith. The full conviction of these things belongs to a later period of his life; but probably, during his first voyagings in the Mediterranean, there hung in his mind echoes of psalms and prophecies that had to do with things beyond the world of his vision and experience. The sun, whose going forth is to the end of heaven, his circuit back to the end of it, and from whose heat there is nothing hid; the truth, holy and prevailing, that knows no speech nor language where its voice is not heard; the great and wide sea, with its creeping things innumerable, and beasts small and great—no wonder if these things impressed him, and if gradually, as his way fell clearer before him, and the inner light began to shine more steadily, he came to believe that he had a special mission to carry the torch of the faith across the Sea of Darkness, and be himself the bearer of a truth that was to go through all the earth, and of words that were to travel to the world's end.

In this faith, then, and with this equipment, and about the year 1465, Christopher Columbus began his sea travels. His voyages would be doubtless at first much along the coasts, and across to Alexandria and the Islands. There would be returnings to Genoa, and glad welcomings by the little household in the narrow street; in 1472 and 1473 he was with his father at Savona, helping with the wool-weaving and tavern-keeping; possibly also there were interviews with Benincasa, who was at that time living in Genoa, and making his famous sea-charts. Perhaps it was in his studio that Christopher first saw a chart, and first fell in love with the magic that can transfer the shapes of oceans and continents to a piece of paper. Then he would be off again in another ship, to the Golden Horn perhaps, or the Black Sea, for the Genoese had a great Crimean trade. This is all conjecture, but very reasonable conjecture; what we know for a fact is that he saw the white gum drawn from the lentiscus shrubs in Chio at the time of their flowering; that fragrant memory is preserved long afterwards in his own writings, evoked by some incident in the newly-discovered islands of the West. There are vague rumours and stories of his having been engaged in various expeditions —among them one fitted out in Genoa by John of Anjou to recover the kingdom of Naples for King Rene of Provence; but there is no reason to believe these rumours: good reason to disbelieve them, rather.

The lives that the sea absorbs are passed in a great variety of adventure and experience, but so far as the world is concerned they are passed in a profound obscurity; and we need not wonder that of all the mariners who used those seas, and passed up and down, and held their course by the stars, and reefed their sails before the sudden squalls that came down from the mountains, and shook them out again in the calm sunshine that followed, there is no record of the one among their number who was afterwards to reef and steer and hold his course to such mighty purpose. For this period, then, we must leave him to the sea, and to the vast anonymity of sea life.

CHAPTER IV

DOMENICO

Christopher is gone, vanished over that blue horizon; and the tale of life in Genoa goes on without him very much as before, except that Domenico has one apprentice less, and, a matter becoming of some importance in the narrow condition of his finances, one boy less to feed and clothe. For good Domenico, alas! is no economist. Those hardy adventures of his in the buying and selling line do not prosper him; the tavern does not pay; perhaps the tavern-keeper is too hospitable; at any rate, things are not going well. And yet Domenico had a good start; as his brother Antonio has doubtless often told him, he had the best of old Giovanni's inheritance; he had the property at Quinto, and other property at Ginestreto, and some ground rents at Pradella; a tavern at Savona, a shop there and at Genoa—really, Domenico has no excuse for his difficulties. In 1445 he was selling land at Quinto, presumably with the consent of old Giovanni, if he was still alive; and if he was not living, then immediately after his death, in the first pride of possession.

In 1450 he bought a pleasant house at Quarto, a village on the sea-shore about a mile to the west of Quinto and about five miles to the east of Genoa. It was probably a pure speculation, as he immediately leased the house for two years, and never lived in it himself, although it was a pleasant place, with an orchard of olives and figs and various other trees—'arboratum olivis ficubus et aliis diversis arboribus'. His next recorded transaction is in 1466, when he went security for a friend, doubtless with disastrous results. In 1473 he sold the house at the Olive Gate, that suburban dwelling where probably Christopher was born, and in 1474 he invested the proceeds of that sale in a piece of land which I have referred to before, situated in the suburbs of Savona, with which were sold those agreeable and useless wine-vats. Domenico was living at Savona then, and the property which he so fatuously acquired consisted of two large pieces of land on the Via Valcalda, containing a few vines, a plantation of fruit-trees, and a large area of shrub and underwood. The price, however, was never paid in full, and was the cause of a lawsuit which dragged on for forty years, and was finally settled by Don Diego Columbus, Christopher's son, who sent a special authority from Hispaniola.

Owing, no doubt, to the difficulties that this un fortunate purchase plunged him into, Domenico was obliged to mortgage his house at St. Andrew's Gate in the year 1477; and in 1489 he finally gave it up to Jacob Baverelus, the cheese-monger, his son-in-law. Susanna, who had been the witness of his melancholy transactions for so many years, and possibly the mainstay of that declining household, died in 1494; but not, we may hope, before she had heard of the fame of her son Christopher. Domenico, in receipt of a pension from the famous Admiral of the Ocean, and no doubt talking with a deal of pride and inaccuracy about the discovery of the New World, lived on until 1498; when he died also, and vanished out of this world. He had fulfilled a noble destiny in being the father of Christopher Columbus.

CHAPTER V

SEA THOUGHTS

The long years that Christopher Columbus spent at sea in making voyages to and from his home in Genoa, years so blank to us, but to him who lived them so full of life and active growth, were most certainly fruitful in training and equipping him for that future career of which as yet, perhaps, he did not dream. The long undulating waves of the Mediterranean, with land appearing and dissolving away in the morning and evening mists, the business of ship life, harsh and rough in detail, but not too absorbing to the mind of a common mariner to prevent any thoughts he might have finding room to grow and take shape; sea breezes, sea storms, sea calms; these were the setting of his knowledge and experience as he fared from port to port and from sea to sea. He is a very elusive figure in that environment of misty blue, very hard to hold and identify, very shy of our scrutiny, and inaccessible even to our speculation. If we would come up with him, and place ourselves in some kind of sympathy with the thoughts that were forming in his brain, it is necessary that we should, for the moment, forget much of what we know of the world, and assume the imperfect knowledge of the globe that man possessed in those years when Columbus was sailing the Mediterranean.

That the earth was a round globe of land and water was a fact that, after many contradictions and uncertainties, intelligent men had by this time accepted. A conscious knowledge of the world as a whole had been a part of human thought for many hundreds of years; and the sphericity of the earth had been a theory in the sixth century before Christ. In the fourth century Aristotle had watched the stars and eclipses; in the third century Eratosthenes had measured a degree of latitude, and measured it wrong;—[Not so very wrong. D.W.]—in the second century the philosopher Crates had constructed a rude sort of globe, on which were marked the known kingdoms of the earth, and some also unknown. With the coming of the Christian era the theory of the roundness of the earth began to be denied; and as knowledge and learning became gathered into the hands of the Church they lost something of their clarity and singleness, and began to be used arbitrarily as evidence for or against other and less material theories. St. Chrysostom opposed the theory of the earth's roundness; St. Isidore taught it; and so also did St. Augustine, as we might expect from a man of his wisdom who lived so long in a monastery that looked out to sea from a high point, and who wrote the words 'Ubi magnitudo, ibi veritas'. In the sixth century of the Christian era Bishop Cosmas gave much thought to this matter of a round world, and found a new argument which to his mind (poor Cosmas!)

disposed of it very clearly; for he argued that, if the world were round, the people dwelling at the antipodes could not see Christ at His coming, and that therefore the earth was not round. But Bede, in the eighth century, established it finally as a part of human knowledge that the earth and all the heavenly bodies were spheres, and after that the fact was not again seriously disputed.

What lay beyond the frontier of the known was a speculation inseparable from the spirit of exploration. Children, and people who do not travel, are generally content, when their thoughts stray beyond the paths trodden by their feet, to believe that the greater world is but a continuation on every side of their own environment; indeed, without the help of sight or suggestion, it is almost impossible to believe anything else. If you stand on an eminence in a great plain and think of the unseen country that lies beyond the horizon, trying to visualise it and imagine that you see it, the eye of imagination can only see the continuance or projection of what is seen by the bodily sight. If you think, you can occupy the invisible space with a landscape made up from your own memory and knowledge: you may think of mountain chains and rivers, although there are none visible to your sight, or you may imagine vast seas and islands, oceans and continents. This, however, is thought, not pure imagination; and even so, with every advantage of thought and knowledge, you will not be able to imagine beyond your horizon a space of sea so wide that the farther shore is invisible, and yet imagine the farther shore also. You will see America across the Atlantic and Japan across the Pacific; but you cannot see, in one single effort of the imagination, an Atlantic of empty blue water stretching to an empty horizon, another beyond that equally vast and empty, another beyond that, and so on until you have spanned the thousand horizons that lie between England and America. The mind, that is to say, works in steps and spans corresponding to the spans of physical sight; it cannot clear itself enough from the body, or rise high enough beyond experience, to comprehend spaces so much vaster than anything ever seen by the eye of man. So also with the stretching of the horizon which bounded human knowledge of the earth. It moved step by step; if one of Prince Henry's captains, creeping down the west coast of Africa, discovered a cape a hundred miles south of the known world, the most he could probably do was to imagine that there might lie, still another hundred miles farther south, another cape; to sail for it in faith and hope, to find it, and to imagine another possibility yet another hundred miles away. So far as experience went back, faith could look forward. It is thus with the common run of mankind; yesterday's march is the measure of to-morrow's; as much as they have done once, they may do again; they fear it will be not much more; they hope it may be not much less.

The history of the exploration of the world up to the day when Columbus set sail from Palos is just such a history of steps. The Phoenicians coasting from harbour to harbour through the Mediterranean; the Romans marching from camp to camp, from country to country; the Jutes venturing in their frail craft into the stormy northern seas, making voyages a little longer and more daring every time, until they reached England; the captains of Prince Henry of Portugal feeling their way from voyage to voyage down the coast of Africa—there are no bold flights into the incredible here, but patient and business-like progress from one stepping-stone to another. Dangers and hardships there were, and brave followings of the faint will-o'-the-wisp of faith in what lay beyond; but there were no great launchings into space. They but followed a line that was the continuance or projection of the line they had hitherto followed; what they did was brave and glorious, but it was reasonable. What Columbus did, on the contrary, was, as we shall see later, against all reason and knowledge. It was a leap in the dark towards some star invisible to all but him; for he who sets forth across the desert sand or sea must have a brighter sun to guide him than that which sets and rises on the day of the small man.

Our familiarity with maps and atlases makes it difficult for us to think of the world in other terms than those of map and diagram; knowledge and science have focussed things for us, and our imagination has in consequence shrunk. It is almost impossible, when thinking of the earth as a whole, to think about it except as a picture drawn, or as a small globe with maps traced upon it. I am sure that our imagination has a far narrower angle—to borrow a term from the science of lenses—than the imagination of men who lived in the fifteenth century. They thought of the world in its actual terms—seas, islands, continents, gulfs, rivers, oceans. Columbus had seen maps and charts—among them the famous 'portolani' of Benincasa at Genoa; but I think it unlikely that he was so familiar with them as to have adopted their terms in his thoughts about the earth. He had seen the Mediterranean and sailed upon it before he had seen a chart of it; he knew a good deal of the world itself before he had seen a map of it. He had more knowledge of the actual earth and sea than he had of pictures or drawings of them; and therefore, if we are to keep in sympathetic touch with him, we must not think too closely of maps, but of land and sea themselves.

The world that Columbus had heard about as being within the knowledge of men extended on the north to Iceland and Scandinavia, on the south to a cape one hundred miles south of the Equator, and to the east as far as China and Japan. North and South were not important to the spirit of that time; it was East and West that men thought of when they thought of the expansion and the discovery of the world. And although they admitted that the earth was a sphere, I think it likely that they imagined (although the imagination was contrary to their knowledge) that the line of West and East was far longer, and full of vaster possibilities, than that of North and South. North was familiar ground to them—one voyage to England, another to Iceland, another to Scandinavia; there was nothing impossible about that. Southward was another matter; but even here there was no ambition to discover the limit of the world. It is an error continually made by the biographers of Columbus that the purpose of Prince Henry's explorations down the coast of Africa was to find a sea road to the West Indies by way of the East. It was nothing of the kind. There was no idea in the minds of the Portuguese of the land which Columbus discovered, and which we now know as the West Indies. Mr. Vignaud contends that the confusion arose from the very loose way in which the term India was applied in the Middle Ages. Several Indias were recognised. There was an India beyond the Ganges; a Middle India between the Ganges and the Indus; and a Lesser India, in which were included Arabia, Abyssinia, and the countries about the Red Sea. These divisions were, however, quite vague, and varied in different periods. In the time of Columbus the word India meant the kingdom of Prester John, that fabulous monarch who had been the subject of persistent legends since the twelfth century; and it was this India to which the Portuguese sought a sea road. They had no idea of a barrier cape far to the south, the doubling of which would open a road for them to the west; nor were they, as Mr. Vignaud believes, trying to open a route for the spice trade with the Orient. They had no great spice trade, and did not seek more; what they did seek was an extension of their ordinary trade with Guinea and the African coast. To the maritime world of the fifteenth century, then, the South as a geographical region and as a possible point of discovery had no attractions.

To the west stretched what was known as the Sea of Darkness, about which even the cool knowledge of the geographers and astronomers could not think steadily. Nothing was known about it, it did not lead anywhere, there were no people there, there was no trade in that direction. The tides of history and of life avoided it; only now and then some terrified mariner, blown far out of his course, came back with tales of sea monsters and enchanted disappearing islands, and shores that receded, and coasts upon which no one could make a landfall. The farthest land known to the west was the Azores; beyond that stretched a vague and impossible ocean of terror and darkness, of which the Arabian writer Xerif al Edrisi, whose countrymen were the sea-kings of the Middle Ages, wrote as follows:

"The ocean encircles the ultimate bounds of the inhabited earth, and all beyond it is unknown. No one has been able to verify anything concerning it, on account of its difficult and perilous navigation, its great obscurity, its profound depth, and frequent tempests; through fear of its mighty fishes and its haughty winds; yet there are many islands in it, some peopled, others uninhabited. There is no mariner who dares to enter into its deep waters; or if any have done so, they have merely kept along its coasts, fearful of departing from them. The waves of this ocean, although they roll as high as mountains, yet maintain themselves without breaking; for if they broke it would be impossible for a ship to plough them."

It is another illustration of the way in which discovery and imagination had hitherto gone by steps and not by flights, that geographical knowledge reached the islands of the Atlantic (none of which were at a very great distance from the coast of Europe or from each other) at a comparatively early date, and stopped there until in Columbus there was found a man with faith strong enough to make the long flight beyond them to the unknown West. And yet the philosophers, and later the cartographers, true to their instinct for this pedestrian kind of imagination, put mythical lands and islands to the westward of the known islands as though they were really trying to make a way, to sink stepping stones into the deep sea that would lead their thoughts across the unknown space. In the Catalan map of the world, which was the standard example of cosmography in the early days of Columbus, most of these mythical islands are marked. There was the island of Antilia, which was placed in 25 deg. 35' W., and was said to have been discovered by Don Roderick, the last of the Gothic kings of Spain, who fled there after his defeat by the Moors. There was the island of the Seven Cities, which is sometimes identified with this Antilia, and was the object of a persistent belief or superstition on the part of the inhabitants of the Canary Islands. They saw, or thought they saw, about ninety leagues to the westward, an island with high peaks and deep valleys. The vision was intermittent; it was only seen in very clear weather, on some of those pure, serene days of the tropics when in the clear atmosphere distant objects appear to be close at hand. In cloudy, and often in clear weather also, it was not to be seen at all; but the inhabitants of the Canaries, who always saw it in the same place, were so convinced of its reality that they petitioned the King of Portugal to allow them to go and take possession of it; and several expeditions were in fact despatched, but none ever came up with that fairy land. It was called the island of the Seven Cities from a legend of seven bishops who had fled from Spain at the time of the Moorish conquest, and, landing upon this island, had founded there seven splendid cities. There was the island of St. Brandan, called after the Saint who set out from Ireland in the sixth century in search of an island which always receded before his ships; this island was placed several hundred miles to the west of the Canaries on maps and charts through out the fifteenth and sixteenth centuries. There was the island of Brazil, to the west of Cape St. Vincent; the islands of Royllo, San Giorgio, and Isola di Mam; but they were all islands of dreams, seen by the eyes of many mariners in that imaginative time, but never trodden by any foot of man. To Columbus, however, and the mariners of his day, they were all real places, which a man might reach by special good fortune or heroism, but which, all things considered, it was not quite worth the while of any man to attempt to reach. They have all disappeared from our charts, like the Atlantis of Plato, that was once charted to the westward of the Straits of Gibraltar, and of which the Canaries were believed to be the last peaks unsubmerged.

Sea myths and legends are strange things, and do not as a rule persist in the minds of men unless they have had some ghostly foundation; so it is possible that these fabled islands of the West were lands that had actually been seen by living eyes, although their position could never be properly laid down nor their identity assured. Of all the wandering seamen who talked in the wayside taverns of Atlantic seaports, some must have had strange tales to tell; tales which sometimes may have been true, but were never believed. Vague rumours hung about those shores, like spray and mist about a headland, of lands seen and lost again in the unknown and uncharted ocean. Doubtless the lamp of faith, the inner light, burned in some of these storm-tossed men; but all they had was a glimpse here and there, seen for a moment and lost again; not the clear sight of faith by which Columbus steered his westward course.

The actual outposts of western occupation, then, were the Azores, which were discovered by Genoese sailors in the pay of Portugal early in the fourteenth century; the Canaries, which had been continuously discovered and rediscovered since the Phoenicians occupied them and Pliny chose them for his Hesperides; and Madeira, which is believed to have been discovered by an Englishman under the following very romantic and moving circumstances.

In the reign of Edward the Third a young man named Robert Machin fell in love with a beautiful girl, his superior in rank, Anne Dorset or d'Urfey by name. She loved him also, but her relations did not love him; and therefore they had Machin imprisoned upon some pretext or other, and forcibly married the young lady to a nobleman who had a castle on the shores of the Bristol Channel.

The marriage being accomplished, and the girl carried away by her bridegroom to his seat in the West, it was thought safe to release Machin. Whereupon he collected several friends, and they followed the newly-married couple to Bristol and laid their plans for an abduction. One of the friends got himself engaged as a groom in the service of the unhappy bride, and found her love unchanged, and if possible increased by the present misery she was in. An escape was planned; and one day, when the girl and her groom were riding in the park, they set spurs to their horses, and galloped off to a place on the shores of the Bristol Channel where young Robert had a boat on the beach and a ship in the offing. They set sail immediately, intending to make for France, where the reunited lovers hoped to live happily; but it came on to blow when they were off the Lizard, and a southerly gale, which lasted for thirteen days, drove them far out of their course.

The bride, from her joy and relief, fell into a state of the gloomiest despondency, believing that the hand of God was turned against her, and that their love would never be enjoyed. The tempest fell on the fourteenth day, and at the break of morning the sea-worn company saw trees and land ahead of them. In the sunrise they landed upon an island full of noble trees, about which flights of singing birds were hovering, and in which the sweetest fruits, the most lovely flowers, and the purest and most limpid waters abounded. Machin and his bride and their friends made an encampment on a flowery meadow in a sheltered valley, where for three days they enjoyed the sweetness and rest of the shore and the companionship of all kinds of birds and beasts, which showed no signs of fear at their presence. On the third day a storm arose, and raged for a night over the island; and in the morning the adventurers found that their ship was nowhere to be seen. The despair of the little company was extreme, and was increased by the condition of poor Anne, upon whom terror and remorse again fell, and so preyed upon her mind that in three days she was dead. Her lover, who had braved so much and won her so gallantly, was turned to stone by this misfortune. Remorse and aching desolation oppressed him; from the moment of her death he scarcely ate nor spoke; and in five days he also was dead, surely of a broken heart. They buried him beside his mistress under a spreading tree, and put up a wooden cross there, with a prayer that any Christians who might come to the island would build a chapel to Jesus the Saviour. The rest of the party then repaired their little boat and put to sea; were cast upon the coast of Morocco, captured by the Moors, and thrown into prison. With them in prison was a Spanish pilot named Juan de Morales, who listened attentively to all they could tell him about the situation and condition of the island, and who after his release communicated what he knew to Prince Henry of Portugal. The island of Madeira was thus rediscovered in 1418, and in 1425 was colonised by Prince Henry, who appointed as Governor Bartolomeo de Perestrello, whose daughter was afterwards to become the wife of Columbus.

So much for the outposts of the Old World. Of the New World, about the possibility of which Columbus is beginning to dream as he sails the Mediterranean, there was no knowledge and hardly any thought. Though new in the thoughts of Columbus, it was very old in itself; generations of men had lived and walked and spoken and toiled there, ever since men came upon the earth; sun and shower, the thrill of the seasons, birth and life and death, had been visiting it for centuries and centuries. And it is quite possible that, long before even the civilisation that produced Columbus was in its dawn, men from the Old World had journeyed there. There are two very old fragments of knowledge which indicate at least the possibility of a Western World of which the ancients had knowledge. There is a fragment, preserved from the fourth century before Christ, of a conversation between Silenus and Midas, King of Phrygia, in which Silenus correctly describes the Old World—Europe, Asia, and Africa—as being surrounded by the sea, but also describes, far to the west of it, a huge island, which had its own civilisation and its own laws, where the animals and the men were of twice our stature, and lived for twice our years. There is also the story told by Plato of the island of Atlantis, which was larger than Africa and Asia together, and which in an earthquake disappeared beneath the waves, producing such a slime upon the surface that no ship was able to navigate the sea in that place. This is the story which the priests of Sais told to Solon, and which was embodied in the sacred inscriptions in their temples. It is strange that any one should think of this theory of the slime who had not seen or heard of the Sargasso Sea—that great bank of floating seaweed that the ocean currents collect and retain in the middle of the basin of the North Atlantic.

The Egyptians, the Tartars, the Canaanites, the Chinese, the Arabians, the Welsh, and the Scandinavians have all been credited with the colonisation of America; but the only race from the Old World which had almost certainly been there were the Scandinavians. In the year 983 the coast of Greenland was visited by Eric the Red, the son of a Norwegian noble, who was banished for the crime of murder. Some fifteen years later Eric's son Lief made an expedition with thirty-five men and a ship in the direction of the new land. They came to a coast where there were nothing but ice mountains having the appearance of slate; this country they named Helluland—that is, Land of Slate. This country is our Newfoundland. Standing out to sea again, they reached a level wooded country with white sandy cliffs, which they called Markland, or Land of Wood, which is our Nova Scotia. Next they reached an island east of Markland, where they passed the winter, and as one of their number who had wandered some distance inland had found vines and grapes, Lief named the country Vinland or Vine Land, which is the country we call New England. The Scandinavians continued to make voyages to the West and South; and finally Thorfinn Karlsefne, an Icelander, made a great expedition in the spring of 1007 with ships and material for colonisation. He made much progress to the southwards, and the Icelandic accounts of the climate and soil and characteristics of the country leave no doubt that Greenland and Nova Scotia were discovered and colonised at this time.

It must be remembered, however, that then and in the lifetime of Columbus Greenland was supposed to—be a promontory of the coast of Europe, and was not connected in men's minds with a western continent. Its early discovery has no bearing on the significance of Columbus's achievement, the greatness of which depends not on his having been the first man from the Old World to set foot upon the shores of the New, but on the fact that by pure faith and belief in his own purpose he did set out for and arrive in a world where no man of his era or civilisation had ever before set foot, or from which no wanderer who may have been blown there ever returned. It is enough to claim for him the merit of discovery in the true sense of the word. The New World was covered from the Old by a veil of distance, of time and space, of absence, invisibility, virtual non-existence; and he discovered it.

CHAPTER VI

IN PORTUGAL

There is no reason to believe that before his twenty-fifth year Columbus was anything more than a merchant or mariner, sailing before the mast, and joining one ship after another as opportunities for good voyages offered themselves. A change took place later, probably after his marriage, when he began to adapt himself rapidly to a new set of surroundings, and to show his intrinsic qualities; but all the attempts that have been made to glorify him socially—attempts, it must be remembered, in which he himself and his sons were in after years the leaders—are entirely mistaken. That strange instinct for consistency which makes people desire to see the outward man correspond, in terms of momentary and arbitrary credit, with the inner and hidden man of the heart, has in truth led to more biographical injustice than is fully realised. If Columbus had been the man some of his biographers would like to make him out—the nephew or descendant of a famous French Admiral, educated at the University of Pavia, belonging to a family of noble birth and high social esteem in Genoa, chosen by King Rene to be the commander of naval expeditions, learned in scientific lore, in the classics, in astronomy and in cosmography, the friend and correspondent of Toscanelli and other learned scientists—we should find it hard indeed to forgive him the shifts and deceits that he practised. It is far more interesting to think of him as a common craftsman, of a lowly condition and poor circumstances, who had to earn his living during the formative period of his life by the simplest and hardest labour of the hand. The qualities that made him what he was were of a very simple kind, and his character owed its strength, not to any complexity or subtlety of training and education, but rather to that very bareness and simplicity of circumstance that made him a man of single rather than manifold ideas. He was not capable of seeing both sides of a question; he saw only one side. But he came of a great race; and it was the qualities of his race, combined with this simplicity and even perhaps vacancy of mind, that gave to his idea, when once the seed of it had lodged in his mind, so much vigour in growth and room for expansion. Think of him, then, at the age of twenty-five as a typical plebeian Genoese, bearing all the characteristic traits of his century and people—the spirit of adventure, the love of gold and of power, a spirit of mysticism, and more than a touch of crafty and elaborate dissimulation, when that should be necessary.

He had been at sea for ten or eleven years, making voyages to and from Genoa, with an occasional spell ashore and plunge into the paternal affairs, when in the year 1476 he found himself on board a Genoese vessel which formed one of a convoy going, to

Lisbon. This convoy was attacked off Cape St. Vincent by Colombo, or Colomb, the famous French corsair, of whom Christopher himself has quite falsely been called a relative. Only two of the Genoese vessels escaped, and one of these two was the ship which carried Columbus. It arrived at Lisbon, where Columbus went ashore and took up his abode.

This, so far as can be ascertained, is the truth about the arrival of Columbus in Portugal. The early years of an obscure man who leaps into fame late in life are nearly always difficult to gather knowledge about, because not only are the annals of the poor short and simple and in most cases altogether unrecorded, but there is always that instinct, to which I have already referred, to make out that the circumstances of a man who late in life becomes great and remarkable were always, at every point in his career, remarkable also. We love to trace the hand of destiny guiding her chosen people, protecting them from dangers, and preserving them for their great moment. It is a pleasant study, and one to which the facts often lend themselves, but it leads to a vicious method of biography which obscures the truth with legends and pretences that have afterwards laboriously to be cleared away. It was so in the case of Columbus. Before his departure on his first voyage of discovery there is absolutely no temporary record of him except a few dates in notarial registers. The circumstances of his life and his previous conditions were supplied afterwards by himself and his contemporaries; and both he and they saw the past in the light of the present, and did their best to make it fit a present so wonderful and miraculous. The whole trend of recent research on the subject of Columbus has been unfortunately in the direction of proving the complete insincerity of his own speech and writings about his early life, and the inaccuracy of Las Casas writings his contemporary biographer, and the first historian of the West Indies. Those of my readers, then, who are inclined to be impatient with the meagreness of the facts with which I am presenting them, and the disproportionate amount of theory to fact with regard to these early years of Columbus, must remember three things. First, that the only record of the early years of Columbus was written long after those years had passed away, and in circumstances which did not harmonise with them; second, that there is evidence, both substantive and presumptive, that much of those records, even though it came from the hands of Columbus and his friends, is false and must be discarded; and third, that the only way in which anything like the truth can be arrived at is by circumstantial and presumptive evidence with regard to dates, names, places, and events upon which the obscure life of Columbus impinged. Columbus is known to have written much about himself, but very little of it exists or remains in his own handwriting. It remains in the form of quotation by others, all of whom had their reasons for not representing quite accurately what was, it must be feared, not even itself a candid and accurate record. The evidence for these very serious statements is the subject of numberless volumes and monographs, which cannot be quoted here; for it is my privilege to reap the results, and not to reproduce the material, of the immense research and investigation to which in the last fifty years the life of Columbus has been subjected.

We shall come to facts enough presently; in the meantime we have but the vaguest knowledge of what Columbus did in Lisbon. The one technical possession which he obviously had was knowledge of the sea; he had also a head on his shoulders, and plenty of judgment and common sense; he had likely picked up some knowledge of cartography in his years at Genoa, since (having abandoned wool-weaving) he probably wished to make progress in the profession of the sea; and it is, therefore, believed that he picked up a living in Lisbon by drawing charts and maps. Such a living would only be intermittent; a fact that is indicated by his periodic excursions to sea again, presumably when funds were exhausted. There were other Genoese in Lisbon, and his own brother Bartholomew was with him there for a time. He may actually have been there when Columbus arrived, but it was more probable that Columbus, the pioneer of the family, seeing a better field for his brother's talent in Lisbon than in Genoa, sent for him when he himself was established there. This Bartholomew, of whom we shall see a good deal in the future, is merely an outline at this stage of the story; an outline that will later be filled up with human features and fitted with a human character; at present he is but a brother of Christopher, with a rather bookish taste, a better knowledge of cartography than Christopher possessed, and some little experience of the book-selling trade. He too made charts in Lisbon, and sold books also, and no doubt between them the efforts of the brothers, supplemented by the occasional voyages of Christopher, obtained them a sufficient livelihood. The social change, in the one case from the society of Genoese wool-weavers, and in the other from the company of merchant sailors, must have been very great; for there is evidence that they began to make friends and acquaintances among a rather different class than had been formerly accessible to them. The change to a new country also and to a new language makes a deep impression at the age of twenty-five; and although Columbus in his sea-farings had been in many ports, and had probably picked up a knowledge both of Portuguese and of Spanish, his establishment in the Portuguese capital could not fail to enlarge his outlook upon life.

There is absolutely no record of his circumstances in the first year of his life at Lisbon, so we may look once more into the glass of imagination and try to find a picture there. It is very dim, very minute, very, very far away. There is the little shop in a steep Lisbon street, somewhere near the harbour we may be sure, with the shadows of the houses lying sharp on the white sunlight of the street; the cool darkness of the shop, with its odour of vellum and parchment, its rolls of maps and charts; and somewhere near by the sounds and commotion of the wharves and the shipping. Often, when there was a purchaser in the shop, there would be talk of the sea, of the best course from this place to that, of the entrance to this harbour and the other; talk of the western islands too, of the western ocean, of the new astrolabe which the German Muller of Konigsberg, or Regiomontanus, as they called him in Portugal, had modified and improved. And if there was sometimes an evening walk, it would surely be towards the coast or on a hill above the harbour, with a view of the sun being quenched in the sea and travelling down into the unknown, uncharted West.

CHAPTER VII

ADVENTURES BODILY AND SPIRITUAL

Columbus had not been long in Portugal before he was off again to sea, this time on a longer voyage than any he had yet undertaken. Our knowledge of it depends on his own words as reported by Las Casas, and, like so much other knowledge similarly recorded, is not to be received with absolute certainty; but on the whole the balance of probability is in favour of its truth. The words in which this voyage is recorded are given as a quotation from a letter of Columbus, and, stripped of certain obvious interpolations of the historian, are as follows:—

"In the month of February, and in the year 1477, I navigated as far as the island of Tile [Thule], a hundred leagues; and to this island, which is as large as England, the English, especially those of Bristol, go with merchandise; and when I was there the sea was not frozen over, although there were very high tides, so much so that in some parts the sea rose twenty-five 'brazas', and went down as much, twice during the day."

The reasons for doubting that this voyage took place are due simply to Columbus's habit of being untruthful in regard to his own past doings, and his propensity for drawing the long bow; and the reason that has been accepted by most of his biographers who have denied the truth of this statement is that, in the year 1492, when Columbus was addressing the King and Queen of Spain on his qualifications as a navigator, and when he wished to set forth his experience in a formidable light, he said nothing about this voyage, but merely described his explorations as having extended from Guinea on the south to England on the north. A shrewd estimate of Columbus's character makes it indeed seem incredible that, if he had really been in Iceland, he should not have mentioned the fact on this occasion; and yet there is just one reason, also quite characteristic of Columbus, that would account for the suppression. It is just possible that when he was at Thule, by which he meant Iceland, he may have heard of the explorations in the direction of Greenland and Newfoundland; and that, although by other navigators these lands were regarded as a part of the continent of Europe, he may have had some glimmerings of an idea that they were part of land and islands in the West; and he was much too jealous of his own reputation as the great and only originator of the project for voyaging to the West, to give away any hints that he was not the only person to whom such ideas had occurred. There is deception and untruth somewhere; and one must make one's choice between regarding the story in the first place as a lie, or accepting it as truth, and putting down Columbus's silence about it on a later occasion to a rare instinct of judicious suppression. There are other facts in his life, to which, we shall come later, that are in accordance with this theory. There is no doubt, moreover, that Columbus had a very great experience of the sea, and was one of the greatest practical seamen, if not the greatest, that has ever lived; and it would be foolish to deny, except for the greatest reasons, that he made a voyage to the far North, which was neither unusual at the time nor a very great achievement for a seaman of his experience.

Christopher returned from these voyages, of which we know nothing except the facts that he has given us, towards the end of 1477; and it was probably in the next year that an event very important in his life and career took place. Hitherto there has been no whisper of love in that arduous career of wool-weaving, sailoring, and map-making; and it is not unlikely that his marriage represents the first inspiration of love in his life, for he was, in spite of his southern birth, a cool-blooded man, for whom affairs of the heart had never a very serious interest. But at Lisbon, where he began to find himself with some footing and place in the world, and where the prospect of at least a livelihood began to open out before him, his thoughts took that turn towards domesticity and family life which marks a moment in the development of almost every man. And now, since he has at last to emerge from the misty environment of sea-spray that has veiled him so long from our intimate sight, we may take a close look at him as he was in this year 1478.

Unlike the southern Italians, he was fair in colouring; a man rather above the middle height, large limbed, of a shapely breadth and proportion, and of a grave and dignified demeanour. His face was ruddy, and inclined to be freckled under the exposure to the sun, his hair at this age still fair and reddish, although in a few years later it turned grey, and became white while he was still a young man. His nose was slightly aquiline, his face long and rather full; his eyes of a clear blue, with sharply defined eyebrows—seamen's eyes, which get an unmistakable light in them from long staring into the sea distances. Altogether a handsome and distinguished-looking young man, noticeable anywhere, and especially among a crowd of swarthy Portuguese. He was not a lively young man; on the contrary, his manner was rather heavy, and even at times inclined to be pompous; he had a very good opinion of himself, had the clear calculating head and tidy intellectual methods of the able mariner; was shrewd and cautious—in a word, took himself and the world very seriously. A strictly conventional man, as the conventions of his time and race went; probably some of his gayer and lighter-hearted contemporaries thought him a dull enough dog, who would not join in a carouse or a gallant adventure, but would probably get the better of you if he could in any commercial deal. He was a great stickler for the observances of religion; and never a Sunday or feast-day passed, when he was ashore, without finding him, like the dutiful son of the Church that he was, hearing Mass and attending at Benediction. Not, indeed, a very attractive or inspiring figure of a man; not the man whose company one would likely have sought very much, or whose conversation one would have found very interesting. A man rather whose character was cast in a large and plain mould, without those many facets which add so much to the brightness of human intercourse, and which attract and reflect the light from other minds; a man who must be tried in large circumstances, and placed in a big setting, if his qualities are to be seen to advantage . . . . I seem to see him walking up from the shop near the harbour at Lisbon towards the convent of Saints; walking gravely and firmly, with a dignified demeanour, with his best clothes on, and glad, for the moment, to be free of his sea acquaintances, and to be walking in the direction of that upper-class world after which he has a secret hankering in his heart. There are a great many churches in Lisbon nearer his house where he might hear Mass on Sundays; but he prefers to walk up to the rich and fashionable convent of Saints, where everybody is well dressed, and where those kindling eyes of his may indulge a cool taste for feminine beauty.

While the chapel bell is ringing other people are hurrying through the sunny Lisbon streets to Mass at the convent. Among the fashionable throng are two ladies, one young, one middle-aged; they separate at the church door, and the younger one leaves her mother and takes her place in the convent choir. This is Philippa Moniz, who lives alone with her mother in Lisbon, and amuses herself with her privileges as a cavaliera, or dame, in one of the knightly orders attached to the rich convent of Saints. Perhaps she has noticed the tall figure of the young Genoese in the strangers' part of the convent, perhaps not; but his roving blue eye has noticed her, and much is to come of it. The young Genoese continues his regular and exemplary attendance at the divine Office, the young lady is zealous in observing her duties in the choir; some kind friend introduces them; the audacious young man makes his proposals, and, in spite of the melancholy protests of the young lady's exceedingly respectable and highly-connected relatives, the young people are betrothed and actually married before the elders have time to recover breath from their first shock at the absurdity of the suggestion.

There is a very curious fact in connection with his marriage that is worthy of our consideration. In all his voluminous writings, letters, memoirs, and journals, Columbus never once mentions his wife. His sole reference to her is in his will, made at Valladolid many years later, long after her death; and is contained in the two words "my wife." He ordains that a chapel shall be erected and masses said for the repose of the souls of his father, his mother, and his wife. He who wrote so much, did not write of her; he who boasted so much, never boasted of her; he who bemoaned so much, never bemoaned her. There is a blank silence on his part about everything connected with his marriage and his wife. I like to think that it was because this marriage, which incidentally furnished him with one of the great impulses of his career, was in itself placid and uneventful, and belongs to that mass of happy days that do not make history. Columbus was not a passionate man. I think that love had a very small place in his life, and that the fever of passion was with him brief and soon finished with; but I am sure he was affectionate, and grateful for any affection and tenderness that were bestowed upon him. He was much away too, at first on his voyages to Guinea and afterwards on the business of his petitions to the Portuguese and Spanish Courts; and one need not be a cynic to believe that these absences did nothing to lessen the affection between him and his wife. Finally, their married life was a short one; she died within ten years, and I am sure did not outlive his affections; so that there may be something solemn, some secret memories of the aching joy and sorrow that her coming into his life and passing out of it brought him, in this silence of Columbus concerning his wife.

This marriage was, in the vulgar idiom of to-day, a great thing for Columbus. It not only brought him a wife; it brought him a home, society, recognition, and a connection with maritime knowledge and adventure that was of the greatest importance to him. Philippa Moniz Perestrello was the daughter of Bartolomeo Perestrello, who had been appointed hereditary governor of the island of Porto Santo on its colonisation by Prince Henry in 1425 and who had died there in 1457. Her grandfather was Gil Ayres Moniz, who was secretary to the famous Constable Pereira in the reign of John I, and is chiefly interesting to us because he founded the chapel of the "Piedad" in the Carmelite Monastery at Lisbon, in which the Moniz family had the right of interment for ever, and in which the body of Philippa, after her brief pilgrimage in this world was over, duly rested; and whence her son ordered its disinterment and re-burial in the church of Santa Clara in San Domingo. Philippa's mother, Isabel Moniz, was the second or third wife of Perestrello; and after her husband's death she had come to live in Lisbon. She had another daughter, Violante by name, who had married one Mulier, or Muliartes, in Huelva; and a son named Bartolomeo, who was the heir to the governorship of Porto Santo; but as he was only a little boy at the time of his father's death his mother ceded the governorship to Pedro Correa da Cunha, who had married Iseult, the daughter of old Bartolomeo by his first wife. The governorship was thus kept in the family during the minority of Bartolomeo, who resumed it later when he came of age.

This Isabel, mother of Philippa, was a very important acquaintance indeed for Columbus. It must be noted that he left the shop and poor Bartholomew to take care of themselves or each other, and went to live in the house of his mother-in-law. This was a great social step for the wool-weaver of Genoa; and it was probably the result of a kind of compromise with his wife's horrified relatives at the time of her marriage. It was doubtless thought impossible for her to go and live over the chart-maker's shop; and as you can make charts in one house as well as another, it was decided that Columbus should live with his mother-in-law, and follow his trade under her roof. Columbus, in fact, seems to have been fortunate in securing the favour of his female relatives-in-law, and it was probably owing to the championship of Philippa's mother that a marriage so much to his advantage ever took place at all. His wife had many distinguished relatives in the neighbourhood of Lisbon; her cousin was archbishop at this very time; but I can neither find that their marriage was celebrated with the archiepiscopal blessing or that he ever got much help or countenance from the male members of the Moniz family. Archbishops even today do not much like their pretty cousins marrying a man of Columbus's position, whether you call him a woolweaver, a sailor, a map-maker, or a bookseller. "Adventurer" is perhaps the truest description of him; and the word was as much distrusted in the best circles in Lisbon in the fifteenth century as it is to-day.

Those of his new relatives, however, who did get to know him soon began to see that Philippa had not made such a bad bargain after all. With the confidence and added belief in himself that the recognition and encouragement of those kind women brought him, Columbus's mind and imagination expanded; and I think it was probably now that he began to wonder if all his knowledge and seamanship, his quite useful smattering of cartography and cosmography, his real love of adventure, and all his dreams and speculations concerning the unknown and uncharted seas, could not be turned to some practical account. His wife's step-sister Iseult and her husband had, moreover, only lately returned to Lisbon from their long residence in Porto Santo; young Bartolomeo Perestrello, her brother, was reigning there in their stead, and no doubt sending home interesting accounts of ships and navigators that put in at Madeira; and all the circumstances would tend to fan the spark of Columbus's desire to have some adventure and glory of his own on the high seas. He would wish to show all these grandees, with whom his marriage had brought him acquainted, that you did not need to be born a Perestrello —or Pallastrelli, as the name was in its original Italian form—to make a name in the world. Donna Isabel, moreover, was never tired of talking about Porto Santo and her dead husband, and of all the voyages and sea adventures that had filled his life. She was obviously a good teller of tales, and had all the old history and traditions of Madeira at her fingers' ends; the story of

Robert Machin and Anne Dorset; the story of the isle of Seven Cities; and the black cloud on the horizon that turned out in the end to be Madeira. She told Christopher how her husband, when he had first gone to Porto Santo, had taken there a litter of rabbits, and how the rabbits had so increased that in two seasons they had eaten up everything on the island, and rendered it uninhabitable for some time.

She brought out her husband's sea-charts, memoranda, and log-books, the sight of which still farther inflamed Christopher's curiosity and ambition. The great thing in those days was to discover something, if it was only a cape down the African coast or a rock in the Atlantic. The key to fame, which later took the form of mechanical invention, and later still of discovery in the region of science, took the form then of actual discovery of parts of the earth's surface. The thing was in the air; news was coming in every day of something new seen, something new charted. If others had done so much, and the field was still half unexplored, could not he do something also? It was not an unlikely thought to occur to the mind of a student of sea charts and horizons.

CHAPTER VIII

THE FIRE KINDLES

The next step in Columbus's career was a move to Porto Santo, which probably took place very soon after his marriage—that is to say, in the year 1479. It is likely that he had the chance of making a voyage there; perhaps even of commanding a ship, for his experience of the sea and skill as a navigator must by this time have raised him above the rank of an ordinary seaman; and in that case nothing would be more natural than that he should take his young wife with him to visit her brother Bartolomeo, and to see the family property. It is one of the charms of the seaman's profession that he travels free all over the world; and if he has no house or other fixed possessions that need to be looked after he has the freedom of the world, and can go where he likes free of cost. Porto Santo and Madeira, lying in the track of the busiest trade on the Atlantic coast, would provide Columbus with an excellent base from which to make other voyages; so it was probably with a heart full of eager anticipation for the future, and sense of quiet happiness in the present, that in the year 1479 Signor Cristoforo Colombo (for he did not yet call himself Senor Cristoval Colon) set out for Porto Santo—a lonely rock some miles north of Madeira. Its southern shore is a long sweeping bay of white sand, with a huddle of sand-hills beyond, and cliffs and peaks of basalt streaked with lava fringing the other shores. When Columbus and his bride arrived there the place was almost as bare as it is to-day. There were the governor's house; the settlement of Portuguese who worked in the mills and sugar-fields; the mills themselves, with the cultivated sugar-fields behind them; and the vineyards, with the dwarf Malmsey vines pegged down to the ground, which Prince Henry had imported from Candia fifty years before. The forest of dragon-trees that had once covered the island was nearly all gone. The wood had all been used either for building, making boats, or for fuel; and on the fruit of the few trees that were left a herd of pigs was fattened. There was frequent communication by boat with Madeira, which was the chief of all the Atlantic islands, and the headquarters of the sugar trade; and Porto Santo itself was a favourite place of call for passing ships. So that it was by no means lonely for Christopher Columbus and his wife, even if they had not had the society of the governor and his settlement.

We can allow him about three years in Porto Santo, although for a part of this time at least he must have been at sea. I think it not unlikely that it was the happiest time of his life. He was removed from the uncomfortable environment of people who looked down upon him because of his obscure birth; he was in an exquisite climate; and living by the sea-shore, as a sailor loves to do; he got on well with Bartolomeo, who was no doubt glad enough of the company of this grave sailor who had seen so much and had visited so many countries; above all he had his wife there, his beautiful, dear, proud Philippa, all to himself, and out of reach of those abominable Portuguese noblemen who paid so much attention to her and so little to him, and made him so jealous; and there was a whispered promise of some one who was coming to make him happier still. It is a splendid setting, this, for the sea adventurer; a charming picture that one has of him there so long ago, walking on the white shores of the great sweeping bay, with the glorious purple Atlantic sparkling and thundering on the sands, as it sparkles and thunders to-day. A place empty and vivid, swept by the mellow winds; silent, but for the continuous roar of the sea; still, but for the scuttling of the rabbits among the sand-hills and the occasional passage of a figure from the mills up to the sugar-fields; but brilliant with sunshine and colour and the bright environment of the sea. It was upon such scenes that he looked during this happy pause in his life; they were the setting of Philippa's dreams and anxieties as the time of motherhood drew near; and it was upon them that their little son first opened his eyes, and with the boom of the Atlantic breakers that he first mingled his small. voice.

It is but a moment of rest and happiness; for Christopher the scene is soon changed, and he must set forth upon a voyage again, while Philippa is left, with a new light in her eyes, to watch over the atom that wakes and weeps and twists and struggles and mews, and sleeps again, in her charge. Sleep well, little son! Yet a little while, and you too shall make voyages and conquests; new worlds lie waiting for you, who are so greatly astonished at this Old World; far journeys by land and sea, and the company of courtiers and kings; and much honour from the name and deeds of him who looked into your eyes with a laugh and, a sob, and was so very large and overshadowing! But with her who quietly sings to you, whose hands soothe and caress you, in whose eyes shines that wonderful light of mother's love—only a little while longer.

While Diego, as this son was christened, was yet only a baby in his cradle, Columbus made an important voyage to the, coast of Guinea as all the western part of the African continent was then called. His solid and practical qualities were by this time beginning to be recognised even by Philippa's haughty family, and it was possibly through the interest of her uncle, Pedro Noronhas, a distinguished minister of the King of Portugal, that he got the command of a caravel in the expedition which set out for Guinea in December 1481. A few miles from Cape Coast Castle, and on the borders of the Dutch colony, there are to-day the ruined remains of a fort; and it is this fort, the fortress of St. George, that the expedition was sent out to erect. On the

11th of December the little fleet set sail for [from? D.W.] Lisbon—ten caravels, and two barges or lighters laden with the necessary masonry and timber-work for the fort. Columbus was in command of one of the caravels, and the whole fleet was commanded by the Portuguese Admiral Azumbaga. They would certainly see Porto Santo and Madeira on their way south, although they did not call there; and Philippa was no doubt looking out for them, and watching from the sand-hills the fleet of twelve ships going by in the offing. They called at Cape Verde, where the Admiral was commissioned to present one of the negro kings with some horses and hawks, and incidentally to obtain his assent to a treaty. On the 19th of January 1482, having made a very good voyage, they, landed just beyond the Cape of the Three Points, and immediately set about the business of the expedition.

There was a state reception, with Admiral Azumbaga walking in front in scarlet and brocade, followed by his captains, Columbus among them, dressed in gorgeous tunics and cloaks with golden collars and, well hidden beneath their finery, good serviceable cuirasses. The banner of Portugal was ceremoniously unfurled and displayed from the top of a tall tree. An altar was erected and consecrated by the chaplain to the expedition, and a mass was sung for the repose of the soul of Prince Henry. The Portugal contingent were then met by Caramansa, the king of the country, who came, surrounded by a great guard of blacks armed with assegais, their bodies scantily decorated with monkey fur and palm leaves. The black monarch must have presented a handsome appearance, for his arms and legs were decked with gold bracelets and rings, he had a kind of dog-collar fitted with bells round his neck, and some pieces of gold were daintily twisted into his beard. With these aids to diplomacy, and doubtless also with the help of a dram or two of spirits or of the wine of Oporto, the treaty was soon concluded, and a very shrewd stroke of business accomplished for the King of Portugal; for it gave him the sole right of exchanging gaudy rubbish from Portugal for the precious gold of Ethiopia. When the contents of the two freight-ships had been unloaded they were beached and broken up by the orders of King John, who wished it to be thought that they had been destroyed in the whirlpools of that dangerous sea, and that the navigation of those rough waters was only safe for the caravels of the Navy. The fort was built in twenty days, and the expedition returned, laden with gold and ivory; Admiral Azumbaga remained behind in command of the garrison.

This voyage, which was a bold and adventurous one for the time, may be regarded as the first recognition of Columbus as a man of importance, for the expedition was manned and commanded by picked men; so it was for all reasons a very fortunate one for him, although the possession of the dangerous secret as to the whereabouts of this valuable territory might have proved to be not very convenient to him in the future.

Columbus went back to Porto Santo with his ambitions thoroughly kindled. He had been given a definite command in the Portuguese Navy; he had been sailing with a fleet; he had been down to the mysterious coast of Africa; he had been trafficking with strange tribes; he had been engaged in a difficult piece of navigation such as he loved; and on the long dreamy days of the voyage home, the caravels furrowing the blue Atlantic before the steady trade-wind, he determined that he would find some way of putting his knowledge to use, and of earning distinction for himself. Living, as he had been lately, in Atlantic seaports overlooking the western ocean it is certain that the idea of discovering something in that direction occupied him more and more. What it was that he was to discover was probably very vague in his mind, and was likely not designated by any name more exact than "lands." In after years he tried to show that it was a logical and scientific deduction which led him to go and seek the eastern shore of the Indian continent by sailing west; but we may be almost certain that at this time he thought of no such thing. He had no exact scientific knowledge at this date. His map making had taught him something, and naturally he had kept his ears open, and knew all the gossip and hearsay about the islands of the West; and there gradually grew in his mind the intuition or conviction—I refuse to call it an opinion—that, over that blue verge of the West, there was land to be found. How this seed of conviction first lodged in his mind it would be impossible to say; in any one of the steps through which we have followed him, it might have taken its root; but there it was, beginning to occupy his mind very seriously indeed; and he began to look out, as all men do who wish to act upon faith or conviction which they cannot demonstrate to another person, for some proofs that his conviction was a sound one.

And now, just at the moment when he needs it most, comes an incident that, to a man of his religious and superstitious habit, seems like the pointing finger of Providence. The story of the shipwrecked pilot has been discredited by nearly all the modern biographers of Columbus, chiefly because it does not fit in with their theory of his scientific studies and the alleged bearing of these on his great discovery; but it is given by Las Casas, who says that it was commonly believed by Columbus's entourage at Hispaniola. Moreover, amid all the tangles of theory and argument in which the achievement of Columbus has been involved, this original story of shipwrecked mariners stands out with a strength and simplicity that cannot be entirely disregarded by the historian who permits himself some light of imagination by which to work. It is more true to life and to nature that Columbus should have received his last impulse, the little push that was to set his accumulated energy and determination in motion, from a thing of pure chance, than that he should have built his achievement up in a logical superstructure resting on a basis of profound and elaborate theory.

In the year following Columbus's return from Guinea, then, he, and probably his family, had gone over to Madeira from Porto Santo, and were staying there. While they were there a small ship put in to Madeira, much battered by storms and bad weather, and manned by a crew of five sick mariners. Columbus, who was probably never far from the shore at Funchal when a ship came into the harbour, happened to see them. Struck by their appearance, and finding them in a quite destitute and grievously invalid condition, he entertained them in his house until some other provision could be made for them. But they were quite worn out. One by one they succumbed to weakness and illness, until one only, a pilot from Huelva, was left. He also was sinking, and when it was obvious that his end was near at hand, he beckoned his good host to his bedside, and, in gratitude for all his kindness, imparted to him some singular knowledge which he had acquired, and with which, if he had lived, he had hoped to win distinction for himself.

The pilot's story, in so far as it has been preserved, and taking the mean of four contemporary accounts of it, was as follows. This man, whose name is doubtful, but is given as Alonso Sanchez, was sailing on a voyage from one of the Spanish ports to England or Flanders. He had a crew of seventeen men. When they had got well out to sea a severe easterly gale sprung up, which drove the vessel before it to the westward. Day after day and week after week, for twenty-eight days, this gale continued. The islands were all left far behind, and the ship was carried into a region far beyond the limits of the ocean marked on the charts. At last they sighted some islands, upon one of which they landed and took in wood and water. The pilot took the bearings of the island, in so far as he was able, and made some observations, the only one of which that has remained being that the natives went naked; and, the wind having changed, set forth on his homeward voyage. This voyage was long and painful. The wind did not hold steady from the west; the pilot and his crew had a very hazy notion of where they were; their dead reckoning was confused; their provisions fell short; and one by one the crew sickened and died until they were reduced to five or six—the ones who, worn out by sickness and famine, and the labours of working the ship short-handed and in their enfeebled condition, at last made the island of Madeira, and cast anchor in the beautiful bay of Funchal, only to die there. All these things we may imagine the dying man relating in snatches to his absorbed listener; who felt himself to be receiving a pearl of knowledge to be guarded and used, now that its finder must depart upon the last and longest voyage of human discovery. Such observations as he had made—probably a few figures giving the bearings of stars, an account of dead reckoning, and a quite useless and inaccurate chart or map—the pilot gave to his host; then, having delivered his soul of its secret, he died. This is the story; not an impossible or improbable one in its main outlines. Whether the pilot really landed on one of the Antilles is extremely doubtful, although it is possible. Superstitious and storm-tossed sailors in those days were only too ready to believe that they saw some of the fabled islands of the Atlantic; and it is quite possible that the pilot simply announced that he had seen land, and that the details as to his having actually set foot upon it were added later. That does not seem to me important in so far as it concerns Columbus. Whether it were true or not, the man obviously believed it; and to the mind of Columbus, possessed with an idea and a blind faith in something which could not be seen, the whole incident would appear in the light of a supernatural sign. The bit of paper or parchment with the rude drawing on it, even although it were the drawing of a thing imagined and not of a thing seen, would still have for him a kind of authority that he would find it hard to ignore. It seems unnecessary to disbelieve this story. It is obviously absurd to regard it as the sole origin of Columbus's great idea; it probably belongs to that order of accidents, small and unimportant in themselves, which are so often associated with the beginnings of mighty events. Walking on the shore at Madeira or Porto Santo, his mind brooding on the great and growing idea, Columbus would remember one or two other instances which, in the light of his growing conviction and know ledge, began to take on a significant hue. He remembered that his wife's relative, Pedro Correa, who had come back from Porto Santo while Columbus was living in Lisbon, had told him about some strange flotsam that came in upon the shores of the island. He had seen a piece of wood of a very dark colour curiously carved, but not with any tool of metal; and some great canes had also come ashore, so big that, every joint would hold a gallon of wine. These canes, which were utterly unlike any thing known in Europe or the islands of the Atlantic, had been looked upon as such curiosities that they had been sent to the King at Lisbon, where they remained, and where Columbus himself afterwards saw them. Two other stories, which he heard also at this time, went to strengthen his convictions. One was the tale of Martin Vincenti, a pilot in the Portuguese Navy, who had found in the sea, four hundred and twenty leagues to the west of Cape St. Vincent, another piece of wood, curiously carved, that had evidently not been laboured with an iron instrument. Columbus also remembered that the inhabitants of the Azores had more than once found upon their coasts the trunks of huge pine-trees, and strangely shaped canoes carved out of single logs; and, most significant of all, the people of Flares had taken from the water the bodies of two dead men, whose faces were of a strange broad shape, and whose features differed from those of any known race of mankind. All these objects, it was supposed, were brought by westerly winds to the shores of Europe; it was not till long afterwards, when the currents of the Atlantic came to be studied, that the presence of such flotsam came to be attributed to the ocean currents, deflected by the Cape of Good Hope and gathered in the Gulf of Mexico, which are sprayed out across the Atlantic.

The idea once fixed in his mind that there was land at a not impossible distance to the west, and perhaps a sea-road to the shores of Asia itself, the next thing to be done, was to go and discover it. Rather a formidable task for a man without money, a foreigner in a strange land, among people who looked down upon him because of his obscure birth, and with no equipment except a knowledge of the sea, a great mastery of the art and craft of seamanship, a fearless spirit of adventure, and an inner light! Some one else would have to be convinced before anything could be done; somebody who would provide ships and men and money and provisions. Altogether rather a large order; for it was not an unusual thing in those days for master mariners, tired of the shore, to suggest to some grandee or other the desirability of fitting out a ship or two to go in search of the isle of St. Brandon, or to look up Antilia, or the island of the Seven Cities. It was very hard to get an audience even for such a reasonable scheme as that; but to suggest taking a flotilla straight out to the west and into the Sea of Darkness, down that curving hill of the sea which it might be easy enough to slide down, but up which it was known that no ship could ever climb again, was a thing that hardly any serious or well-informed person would listen to. A young man from Genoa, without a knowledge either of the classics or of the Fathers, and with no other argument except his own fixed belief and some vague talk about bits of wood and shipwrecked mariners, was not the person to inspire the capitalists of Portugal. Yet the thing had to be done. Obviously it could not be done at Porto Santo, where there were no ships and no money. Influence must be used; and Columbus knew that his proposals, if they were to have even a chance of being listened to, must be presented in some high-flown and elaborate form, giving reasons and offering inducements and quoting authorities. He would have to get some one to help him in that; he would have to get up some scientific facts; his brother Bartholomew could help him, and some of those disagreeable relatives-in-law must also be pressed into the service of the Idea. Obviously the first thing was to go back to Lisbon; which accordingly Columbus did, about the year 1483.

The End

www.ingramcontent.com/pod-product-compliance
Lightning Source LLC
Chambersburg PA
CBHW060005300526
45794CB00003B/1101